VOLUME NUMBER ONE

BIRDS REFERENCE BOOK

AN IMAGE ARCHIVE FOR
ARTISTS *And* DESIGNERS

EDITIONS
Vault

INTRODUCTION

VAULT EDITIONS

Birds are one of the most varied and beautiful creatures on Earth, and they have inspired artists, designers, printmakers and tattoo artists for centuries. Birds are a fantastic and diverse subject for artists and offer a wealth of inspiration and learning opportunities, but what makes birds such an inspiring subject? Their beautiful feathers, made of unique patterns and shapes, and their graceful wings and elegant form are fascinating topics of study for artists looking to expand their knowledge of the animal form. The inspiration birds gift us has added beauty, elegance and meaning to many creative disciplines throughout history, from fine artworks to industrial design, to inspiration for jewellery design or a symbolic element in a tattoo. These animals continue to ignite our imaginations and inspire the great artists of today.

Birds: An Image Archive for Artists and Designers is an essential resource for creatives who want to increase their knowledge of these animals and take their artwork to the next level.

vaulteditions.com

TABLE OF CONTENTS

DOWNLOAD YOUR FILES

Downloading your files is simple. To access your digital files, please go to the last page of this book and follow the instructions.

For technical assistance, please email:
info@vaulteditions.com

BIRDS REFERENCE BOOK

VAULT EDITIONS

BIRDS

BIRDS

BIRDS

BIRDS

31

32

33

34

35

BIRDS

41

42

43

44

BIRDS

45

46

47

48

49

51

50

BIRDS

52

53

BIRDS

56

57

BIRDS

58 59

CATHARTIDAE

BIRDS

60

61

62

63

64

65

66

67

68

BIRDS

69

70

BIRDS

71

72

73

74

75

76

77

78

BIRDS

80

81

82

83

84

85

86

87

BIRDS

BIRDS

BIRDS

90

91

93

94

BIRDS

95

96

97

98

99

100

101

102

103

BIRDS

BIRDS

104

105

106

107

108

109

110

112

111

113

114

115

116

117

118

119

120

121

122

127

128

130

129

131

132

133

134

135

136

137

138

BIRDS

142

141

143

144

145

146

147

148

149

150

156

157

158

159

160

161

162

BIRDS

163

164

165

166

167

168

169

170

171

172

173

174

175

176

177

BIRDS

178

179

180

181

182

183

BIRDS

BIRDS

184

185

186

187

188

189

190

191

194

195

198

199

200

201

202

203

204

205

206

207

212

213

214

215

216   217

218

219

BIRDS

220

ORIOLIDAE

221

222

223

224

225

227

226

228

229

230

231

232

233

234

235

236

237

238

BIRDS

239

240

241

242

243

244

BIRDS

BIRDS

245

246

247

248

249

250

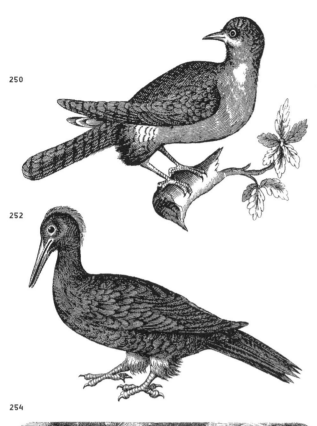

251

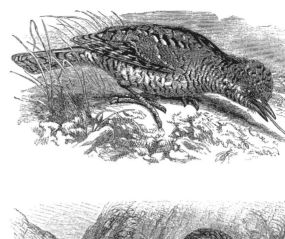

252

253

254

255

BIRDS

<256   257

258

259

260

<261

262

263

264

265

266

267

268

269

270

271

272

273

274

275

276

277

278

280

279

281

282

283

285

284

286

BIRDS

287

288

289

290

291

292

293

294

295

296

BIRDS

299

300

301

303

302

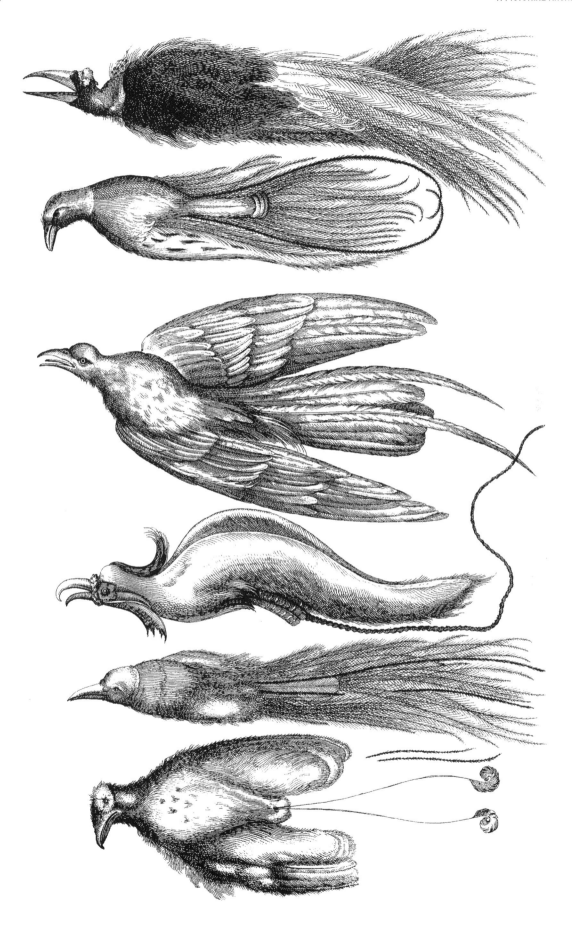

BIRDS

305

306

307

308

310

309

311

312

313

314

315

317

318

319

PHOENICOPTERIDAE

320

321

322

323

324

325

326

327

328

329

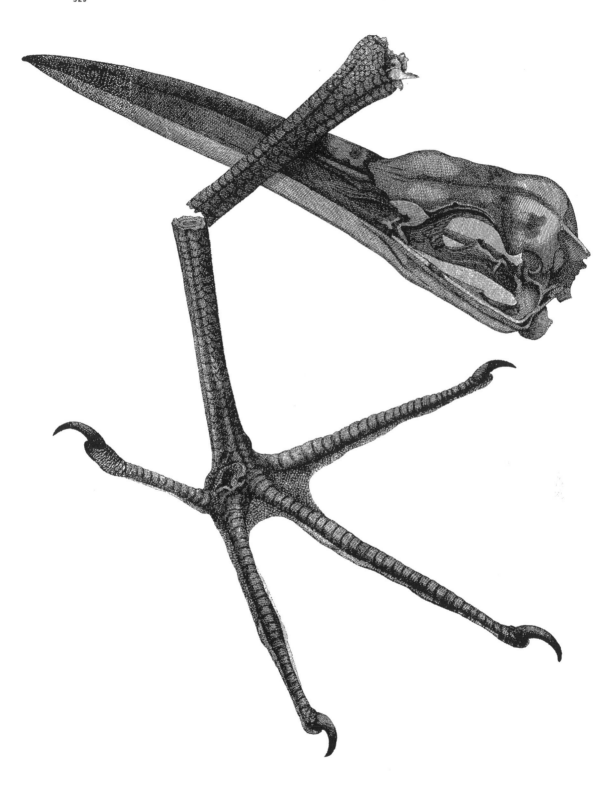

BIRDS

BIRDS

330

331

332

333

334

335

336

BIRDS

337

338

339

340

BIRDS

341

342

ARDEIDAE

343

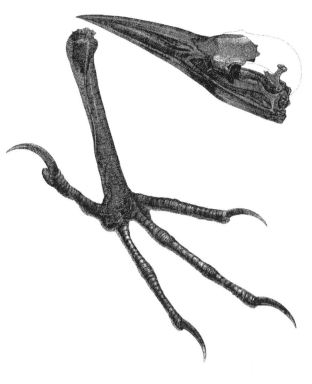

345

346

347

348

349

350

351

352

353

STRUTHIONIDAE

BIRDS

354

355

356

357

358

359

360

361

363

362

364

365

BIRDS

BIRDS

377

378

BIRDS

379

380

381

382

383

384

BIRDS

385

386

BIRDS

417

418

420

421

419

422

BIRDS

LIST OF ILLUSTRATIONS

BIRDS

VAULTEDITIONS.COM

LEARN MORE

At Vault Editions, our mission is to create the world's most diverse and comprehensive collection of image archives available for artists, designers and curious minds. If you have enjoyed this book, you can find more of our titles available at vaulteditions.com.

REVIEW THIS BOOK

As a small, family-owned independent publisher, reviews help spread the word about our work. We would be incredibly grateful if you could leave an honest review of this title wherever you purchased this book.

JOIN OUR COMMUNITY

Are you a creative and curious individual? If so, you will love our community on Instagram. Every day we share bizarre and beautiful artwork ranging from 17th and 18th-century natural history and scientific illustration, to mythical beasts, ornamental designs, anatomical illustration and more. Join our community of 100K+ people today— search @vault_editions on Instagram.

DOWNLOAD YOUR FILES

STEP ONE

Enter the following web address in your web browser on a desktop computer.

www.vaulteditions.com/pages/brb

STEP TWO

Enter the following unique password to access the download page.

brba23648378sxda

STEP THREE

Follow the prompts to access your high-resolution files.

TECHNICAL ASSISTANCE

For all technical assistance, please email: info@vaulteditions.com

Made in the USA
Monee, IL
02 June 2023

1aae49c9-e822-4ea6-917f-fbcf78b8bdb7R01